Buil
Purim

by Joel Lurie
Grishaver
photographs by
Jane Golub, Joel
Lurie Grishaver
and Alan Rowe

Torah Aura Productions
Los Angeles, California

וירי בימי אחשורוש הוא אחשורוש המלך
מהדו ועד כוש שבע ועשרים ומאה מדינה
בימים ההם כשבת המלך אחשורוש על כסא
מלכותו אשר בשושן הבירה בשנת שלוש
למלכו עשה משתה לכל שריו ועבדיו חיל פרס
ומדי הפרתמים ושרי המדינות לפניו בהראתו
את עשר כבוד מלכותו ואת יקר תפארת גדולתו
ימים רבים שמונים ומאת יום ובמלואת הימים
האלה עשה המלך לכל העם הנמצאים בשושן
הבירה למגדול ועד קטן משתה שבעת ימים
בחצר גנת ביתן המלך חור כרפס ותכלת אחוז
בחבלי בוץ וארגמן על גלילי כסף ועמודי שש
מטות זהב וכסף על רצפת בהט ושש ודר וסחרת
והשקות בכלי זהב וכלים מכלים שונים ויין מלכות

For our mothers:
Sally, Dorothy and Doris-
who forced the development of
our senses of humor

Thank You:
Janice & Marvin
Temple Beth El, San Pedro
Valley Beth Shalom, Encino
Stephen S. Wise Synagogue,
Bel Air
The Jewish Quarter,
Beverly Hills
Trevor's Place, Philadelphia

Our Advisory Committee:
Melanie Berman, Sherry
Bissel-Blumberg, Gail Dorph,
Paul Flexner, Frieda
Hirschman-Huberman, Debi
Mahrer, Peninah Schram, &
Joyce Seglin

Our Professional Services:
copyeditor: Carolyn Moore-
Mooso
Tina of Western Costumes
Alef Type and Design
Alan's Custom Lab
Gibbons Color Lab
Inter-Collegiate Press

ISBN #0-933873—12—3

Torah Aura Productions
4423 Fruitland Avenue
Los Angeles, California 90058

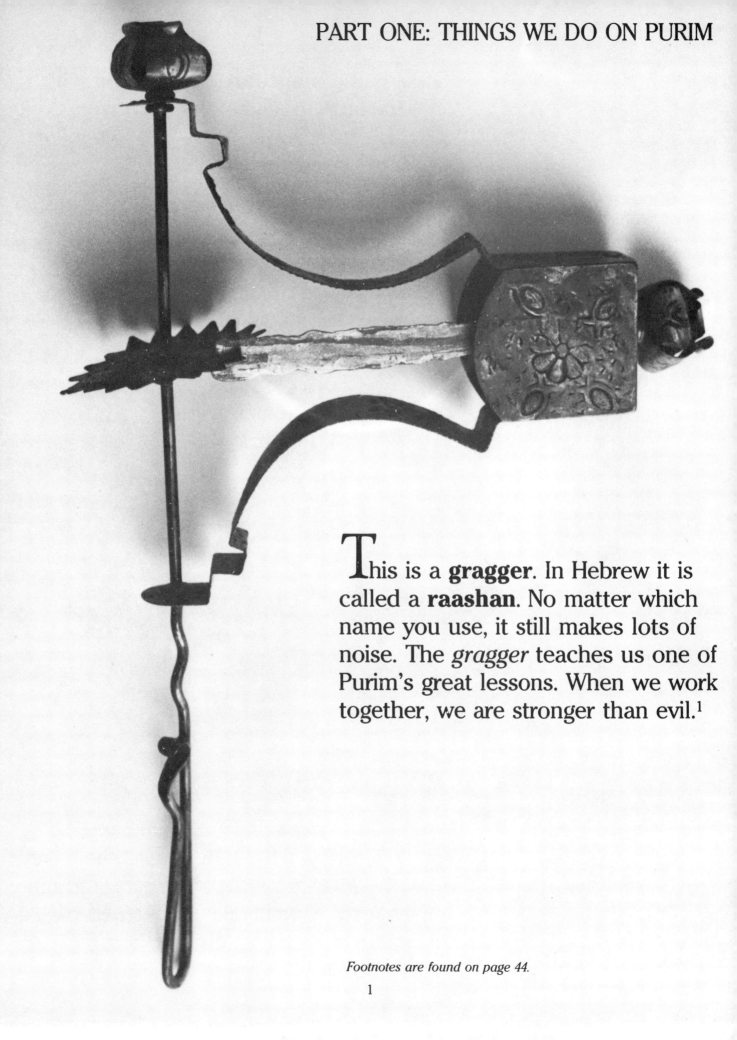

This is a **gragger**. In Hebrew it is called a **raashan**. No matter which name you use, it still makes lots of noise. The *gragger* teaches us one of Purim's great lessons. When we work together, we are stronger than evil.[1]

Footnotes are found on page 44.

1

This is the **megillah**. It is a scroll which tells the story of Queen Esther. Like a *Sefer Torah* (a Torah Scroll), the *megillah* must be written by hand.[2]

Esther was a Jewish woman who became a Queen of Persia. She saved the Jewish people from a wicked man named Haman. Haman wanted to murder every single Jew.[3]

2

ויהי בימי אחשורוש הוא **אחשורוש**
מהדו ועד כוש שבע ועשרים ומאה
ימים הרב כשבת המלך אחשורוש
מלכותו אשר בשושן הבירה בשנת של
למדו עשה משתה לכל שריו ועבדיו חיל
ומדי הפרתמים ושרי המדינות לפניו
את עשר כבוד מלכותו ואת יקר תפארת ג
ימים רבים שמונים ומאת יום ובמלואת ה
האלה עשה המלך לכל העם הנמצאים בש
הבירה למגדול ועד קטן משתה שבעת
בחצר גנת ביתן המלך חור כרפס ותכלת אח
בתלי בוץ וארגמן על גלילי כסף ועמודי ש
מטות זהב וכסף על רצפת בהט ושש ודר וסחר
והשקות בכלי זהב וכלים מכלים שונים ויין מלכו

These are **hamantashen**. They
are special Purim cookies which are
named after Haman. *Hamantashen*
are shaped like triangles. No one is
sure why. Some people think that
Haman wore a three cornered hat.
Other people think that Haman had
big ears which were shaped like
triangles.

When we read the story of Esther from the *megillah*, we make lots of noise every time Haman's name is read. We spin our *gragger*. We shout. We stomp our feet. We make sure than no one can hear the evil name Haman. Together, we can make lots of noise. Together, we are very strong.

Esther was just one Jew, but she saved the whole Jewish people. Her story teaches us that every person can be a hero. Every Jew is important.

Purim is the holiday on which we remember the story of Esther. To make sure that we never forget that every Jew can be like Esther, we make sure that the day on which we tell her story is a day filled with fun.

Purim is a time for parties. Purim is costumes and carnivals. It is noisemakers and *hamantashen*. Purim is reading the *megillah*, acting silly, shouting and making noise, winning prizes, giving *shelaḥ manot* and having the best time.

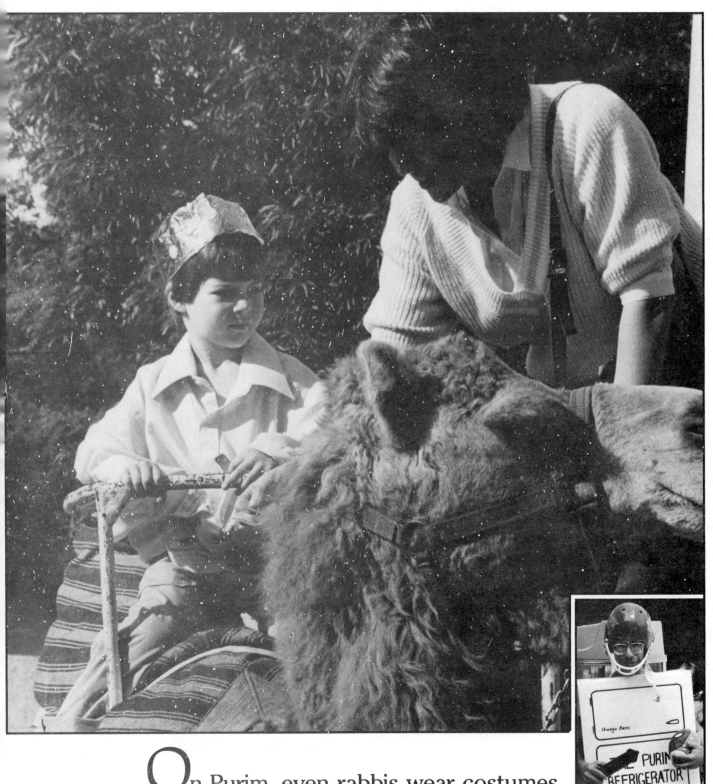

On Purim, even rabbis wear costumes.

F̲our *mitzvot* teach us how to celebrate Purim.[4]

1

2

O̲n Purim, it is a *mitzvah* to **hear** the *megillah* read. It is important to learn from the story of Esther and her cousin Mordechai.

O̲n Purim, it is a *mitzvah* to **give** gifts to your friends. This is called *Shelah Manot*. On the first Purim, Mordechai ordered all Jews to give gifts. Today we still follow his instructions.

3

4

On Purim, it is also a *mitzvah* to **give** gifts to the poor. Mordechai made sure that *tzedakah* gifts were also part of the first Purim. It is an important lesson. Jews try to make *tzedakah* part of every celebration.

On Purim, it is a *mitzvah* to **celebrate** and be happy. Parties, special meals, gifts, *hamantashen*, costumes, carnivals, plays and *graggers* are all part of the Purim celebration.

PART TWO: THE STORY OF ESTHER

The **Purim Spiel** is another way to celebrate and have a good time. It is always fun to make up plays. On Purim we put on a show which tells the story of Mordechai, Esther, King Ahasuerus and Haman.

These are the characters in our Purim Spiel.

THE MEGILLAH READER The person who tells our story.

KING AHASUERUS The King of Persia.

QUEEN VASHTI The first wife of King Ahasuerus.

HAMAN An advisor to the King who is evil.

ESTHER A Jewish woman who becomes the King's queen.

MORDECHAI A wise Jew. Esther's cousin.

MESSENGER A servant who tells the King's decrees to the people.

SERVANT A servant.

ESTHER'S MAID A maid.

BIGTHAN A man who wants to kill the King.

TERESH Another man who wants to kill the King.

10

THE MEGILLAH READER: Once there was a king named Ahasuerus. He ruled over a very big kingdom which went all the way from India, which is in Asia, to Ethiopia, which is in Africa.

Once, King Ahasuerus gave a party for all his advisors, and assistants, and his army. At the same time, Queen Vashti gave a party for all the important women in the kingdom. Both parties went on for seven days.

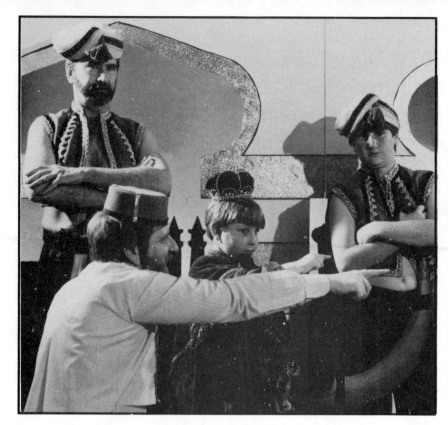
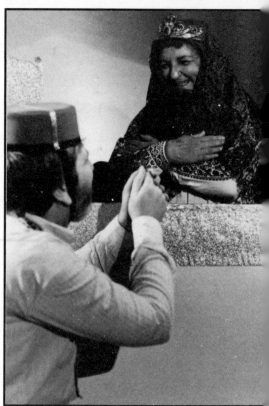

KING AHASUERUS: Send for my Queen, Vashti. Tell her to come to me wearing the royal crown. I want to show off her beauty.

QUEEN VASHTI: No! No way!

KING AHASUERUS: Queen Vashti won't come to my party. What should I do?

ADVISOR: This is a bad thing. After this, every wife in the kingdom will refuse to follow orders. Queen Vashti should no longer be queen.

KING AHASUERUS: Then Vashti is no longer my Queen! Take a decree: From now on in my Kingdom, wives must show respect to their husbands.

MESSENGER: A decree from Ahasuerus the King. From now on, it is a law that all wives must show respect to their husbands.

Pretend:

1. You are invited to spend seven days at King Ahasuerus' party. What kind of things would you do? Think of one joke or riddle you would tell.
2. You are invited to spend seven days at Queen Vashti's party. What would it be like? What would you talk about?
3. Act out a husband and wife hearing King Ahasuerus' decree that all wives must obey their husbands.

Discuss:

Was Ahasuerus a good King?

THE MEGILLAH READER: Time passed. Soon, the King was no longer angry at Vashti. Instead, King Ahasuerus was lonely.

KING AHASUERUS: I don't have a Queen anymore. What should I do?

SERVANT: Look for the most beautiful women in your kingdom. Have all of them brought to your palace in Shushan. Pick the most beautiful to be your new Queen.

MESSENGER: A decree from Ahasuerus the King. The King needs a new queen. All the beautiful women must come to Shushan so that the King can choose a new wife.

Pretend:

1. If you were ordered to go the Palace so that the King might choose you to be his Queen, how would you feel?
2. Act out a conversation between two women who are getting ready to be shown to the King.
3. If you were a King, what would be the most important thing to look for in a new Queen?
4. Act out a conversation between the King and an advisor. Imagine that the King is trying to pick the right woman to be his Queen.

THE MEGILLAH READER:
In Shushan lived a Jewish man named Mordechai. He had a beautiful cousin named Esther. Both her father and mother had died. Mordechai had raised her and acted like her father.

MESSENGER: Esther is a beautiful woman. She must be taken to the King's palace.

MORDECHAI: *(In a whisper.)* Esther, do not tell anyone that you are a Jew.

THE MEGILLAH READER: Esther was taken to the palace. She followed Mordechai's orders. She told no one that she was a Jew.

Every day, Mordechai would walk by the palace gate to make sure that Esther was okay.

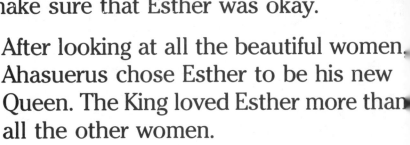

After looking at all the beautiful women, Ahasuerus chose Esther to be his new Queen. The King loved Esther more than all the other women.

Pretend:

1. Imagine that you were Esther. How would it feel to be the only Jewish woman in the palace? Act out Esther talking to herself about life in Ahashuerus' palace.
2. Every day, Mordechai came to the palace to check on Esther. Act out that walk.

Discuss:

Mordechai told Esther to hide the fact that she was a Jew. Was this the right thing to do?

14

THE MEGILLAH READER: Two men, Bigthan and Teresh, worked in the Palace. They were angry at the King. One day when Mordechai was walking by the Palace gate, he heard them talking:

BIGTHAN: I'm angry at the King.

TERESH: I'm angry at him, too. Let's kill him.

THE MEGILLAH READER: Mordechai told Esther, who told the King, who told his guards. The King was saved. Bigthan and Teresh were hung. Mordechai's name was written in the King's official book.

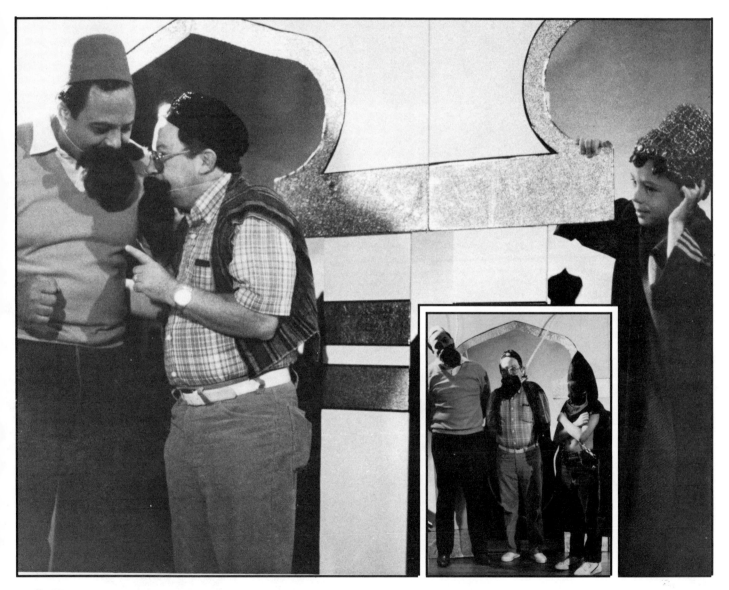

Pretend:

The Megillah doesn't tell us why Bigthan and Teresh wanted to kill the King. Make up a reason why they were that mad at the king.

Discuss:

Are there ever good reasons to kill a king (or anyone else)?

THE MEGILLAH READER: King Ahasuerus had an advisor named Haman. The King made Haman his chief advisor.

MESSENGER: A decree from Ahasuerus the King. Everyone in the palace must bow down to Haman.

THE MEGILLAH READER: But Mordechai refused to bow down.

SERVANT: Why won't you bow down? Why won't you obey the King's command?

MORDECHAI: I am a Jew.

THE MEGILLAH READER: From that day, Haman hated all Jews. He decided to kill them all. He had his servants throw *purim*[5] (lots), to pick the day on which all Jews would die. They chose the 13th of the month of Adar. He then went to the King.

HAMAN: There is a People who live all over your kingdom. They have their own laws. They don't follow all the King's laws. They should all be killed. I will pay you 1,000 pieces of silver if you let me be in charge.

KING AHASUERUS: Here is my royal ring. Keep your money and do what you want to these people.

MESSENGER: A decree from Ahasuerus the King: "On the 13th day of the month of Adar, every Jew in my kingdom should be killed."

KING AHASUERUS: Haman, let's have a drink.

Pretend:

Imagine that you live in Shushan and the King has just ordered everyone to bow down to Haman. What would you do?
Discuss:

1. Why didn't Mordechai bow down to Haman?
2. Mordechai told Esther not to tell anyone that she was a Jew. Then, he told that he was a Jew. Why do you think he told?

THE MEGILLAH READER: When Mordechai heard the King's decree he acted just as if someone had died. He put on sackcloth and ashes. He went out on the streets shouting and crying.

Soon, all the Jews in the Kingdom were fasting, shouting, crying and wearing sackcloth and ashes.

ESTHER'S MAID: Your cousin Mordechai is running all over town in sackcloth and ashes.

ESTHER: Take these new clothes to Mordechai.

THE MEGILLAH READER: But Mordechai would not take the new clothes.

MORDECHAI: Haman has made the King order the killing of all Jews. You must go to the King.

ESTHER: I can't go. No one can go to the King unless he sends for them. Anyone who goes to the King without being invited is killed. Only if the King decides to hold out his gold scepter does the person live.

MORDECHAI: Do not think that you will escape. All Jews will be killed.

ESTHER: I will go to the King. But, you must ask all the Jews in Shushan to fast for three days. My maids and I will also fast.

Pretend:

Imagine you are Esther. Mordechai has told you that you must risk your life to try to save the Jewish people. How would you feel? Act out a conversation between Esther and her maid.

Discuss:

Are there times when you should risk your life? Are there times that you should *not* risk your life?

18

THE MEGILLAH READER: Three days later, Esther went to see the King. She had not been invited. When the King saw her, he tipped his golden scepter. Esther touched it.

KING AHASUERUS: Esther, what do you want? I'll do anything for you. I will even give you half my kingdom.

ESTHER: All I want is to have the King and Haman come to a party.

KING AHASUERUS: Your wish is granted.

THE MEGILLAH READER: The King and Haman came to the party. They had a good time. The King offered Esther another wish.

ESTHER: All I want is to have the King and Haman come to another party.

KING AHASUERUS: Your wish is granted.

THE MEGILLAH READER: When Haman left the party he felt good. He felt special that the Queen had invited him. When Haman walked home he saw Mordechai in the palace gate. Mordechai would not bow down. Haman got angry. He ordered that a huge gallows be built. On the 13th of Adar, Mordechai would hang from that gallows.

THE MEGILLAH READER: That night the King couldn't sleep.

KING AHASUERUS: Bring me my official book. Read it to me. That will put me to sleep.

SERVANT: Mordechai saved the King's life.

KING AHASUERUS: And what was done for him?

SERVANT: Nothing.

THE MEGILLAH READER: The King sent for Haman.

KING AHASUERUS: What should be done for someone the King really wants to honor?

THE MEGILLAH READER: Haman thought the King was going to honor him.

HAMAN: I would have him dressed in the King's best robe with a crown on his head. I would have him placed on the King's horse and led through the streets by one of the King's advisors. I would have the advisor shout: "This is a man the King wants to honor."

KING AHASUERUS: Go and do that for Mordechai.

THE MEGILLAH READER: Haman was not happy.

HAMAN: This is a man the King wants to honor.

Pretend:

How did Haman feel after this happened? Act out a conversation between Haman and his wife. Talk about what happened with the king.

Discuss:

Was Ahasuerus a wicked king?

20

THE MEGILLAH READER: The King and Haman came to Queen Esther's second party.

KING AHASUERUS: Esther, what do you want? I'll do anything for you. I will even give you half my kingdom.

ESTHER: Someone wants to kill me. Please save my life.

KING AHASUERUS: Who is it?

ESTHER: The wicked Haman.

SERVANT: Haman made a huge gallows which he was going to use to hang Mordechai.

KING AHASUERUS: Hang Haman on it!

KING AHASUERUS: I give to Esther everything that used to belong to Haman. I give my royal ring to Mordechai. He can use my power to save the Jews.

MESSENGER: A decree from King Ahashuerus. On the 13th of Adar, Jews should fight to defend themselves.

MORDECHAI: Every year Jews should celebrate the 14th of Adar as a holiday called Purim. They should send gifts to each other, and give *tzedakah* to the poor. They should tell the story of what happened here.

THE MEGILLAH READER: Mordechai, the Jew, became King Ahasuerus' chief advisor. He brought peace to the kingdom.

Pretend:

Now that Haman was gone, Esther and Mordechai were in charge of King Ahashuerus' kingdom. Imagine how the two of them made their plans. Act out a planning session.

Discuss:

The story of Esther is a story of a time when Jews saved themselves. The story of Esther doesn't say anything about God. What do you think God was doing while all this was happening?
What is the message of the story of Esther?

PART THREE: WHAT WE LEARN FROM PURIM

Jews hear the story of Esther every single year. Each time we read it, we have the chance to learn something new. The *megillah* is read out loud in the synagogue. The same as with the Torah, we have to say special *brakhot* before and after reading. Learning from the story of Esther is one of Purim's *mitzvot*.

Haman was a very evil man. We make as much noise as possible whenever his name is read. We don't even want to hear his name. We shout, whistle, spin our *graggers*, and even stomp our feet. Some Jews write Haman's name on the bottom of their shoes. Purim is a time to stamp out evil.

Ever since the first Purim, Jews have sent *shelah manot* to their friends and families. *Shelah manot* is sending small gifts of two different kinds of food. *Shelah manot* is a *mitzvah* which lets you share the joy of Purim with the people you like and love.

There is a second kind of gift we give on Purim. Mordechai also ordered Jews to perform the *mitzvah* of giving *mattanot le-evyonim*, gifts to the poor. Maimonides,[6] a famous Jewish teacher, taught:

A person should spend more money on gifts for the poor than on a Purim dinner or on gifts for friends. The greatest joy comes from making happy the poor, the homeless, and the needy. A person who brings joy to a person who is unhappy is imitating God.

The Laws of Megillah and Hanukkah, 2.77

26

Purim is the happiest day in the Jewish year. We do fun things like going to carnivals, dressing in costumes and having a special Purim Dinner. Being happy on Purim is a *mitzvah*. We remember how heroes like Mordechai and Esther saved the whole Jewish people. We remember that every Jew can be a hero.

PART FOUR: ACTIVITIES

KING AHASUERUS

1. I was King of _____ .
2. I had a Queen who would not do everything I said.
3. Her name was _____ .
4. Then I found a new Queen.
5. Her name was _____ .
6. I loved her very much.
7. I had an advisor named _____ .
8. He was very evil.

Vashti
Haman
Persia
Esther

HAMAN

1. I was an advisor to _____ Ahasuerus.
2. The King made everyone bow down to me.
3. _____ would not do it.
4. He was a _____ .
5. I hated him.
6. I hated all his people.
7. I had the King decree that all Jews would die.

Jew
King
Mordechai

MORDECHAI

1. I was a Jew who lived in the city of _____ .
2. King Ahasuerus made all the beautiful women in the kingdom come to his palace.
3. My cousin _____ had to go.
4. I told her not tell anyone that she was a _____ .
5. She was picked to be Queen.
6. Haman planned to kill all the Jews.
7. I told Esther that she must go to the _____ .

King
Shushan
Esther
Jew

ESTHER

1. My cousin _____ was like a father to me.
2. King _____ chose me to be his Queen.
3. The King loved me very much.
4. My cousin loved me, too.
5. He came to the palace every day to make sure I was okay.
6. _____ planned to kill all the Jews.
7. I was afraid, but I went to see the King.
8. The Jewish people were safe.

Ahasuerus
Haman
Mordechai

Purim is a time to study heroes and heroines. We try to be like Esther and Mordechai. We want to be just like them. We want to be brave and strong, wise and full of faith. Purim is also a good time to talk about heroes.

Spend some time talking about heroes. Use these questions as guidelines. Parents should write down both their own answers and those of their children.

Children should ask their parents:

Who is one of your heroes? _____

What did she or he do? _____

_____ .

How would you like me to be like him or her? _____

_____ .

Parents should ask their children:

Who is one of your heroes? _____

What did she or he do? _____

_____ .

How would you like me to be like him or her? _____

_____ .

HAMANTASHEN

The Dough

3 eggs
1 cup of sugar
3/4 cup of oil
4 cups of flour
4 tsp. baking powder
juice of one orange

1. Beat the eggs.
2. Using a mix-master, add the sugar and beat well.
3. Add the remaining ingredients (oil, flour, baking powder and orange juice) and mix until blended.

The Filling

1 pound pitted prunes
8 ounces of raisins
6 ounces of chopped walnuts
juice of 1/2 lemon
sugar to taste (about 1 teaspoon)

1. Soak prunes and raisins in boiling water for 10 minutes and drain.
2. Finely chop prunes and raisins (or grind in blender or Food Processor).
3. Mix the prune/raisin mixture with the walnuts, lemon juice and sugar.

Making the Hamantashen

1. Roll out small amounts of the dough at a time until 1/4 inch thick. Dough will be soft, so use enough flour on the rolling pin and board so that it doesn't stick.
2. Using a 2 inch round cookie cutter, cut out circles of dough.
3. Place a rounded teaspoon of filling in the center of each circle of dough.
4. Fold up three sides of the circle and pinch the ends to make triangles.
5. Place Hamentashen on a greased cookie sheet.
6. Brush each Hamentashen with beaten egg for a golden finish.
7. Bake 15 minutes at 350 degrees.
8. When finished baking, remove Hamantashen from cookie sheet to cool.

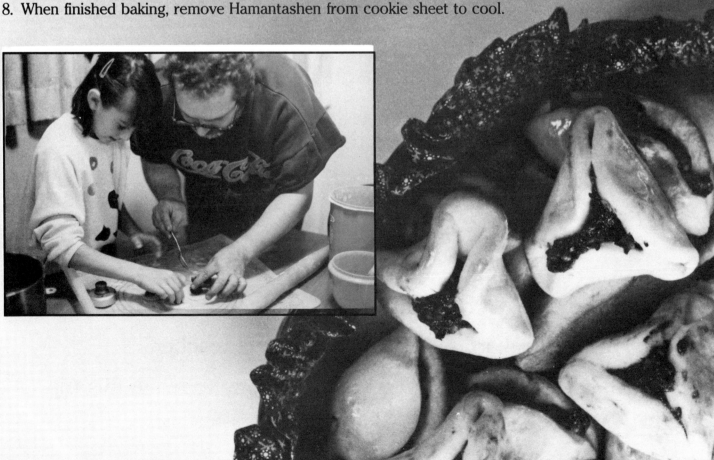

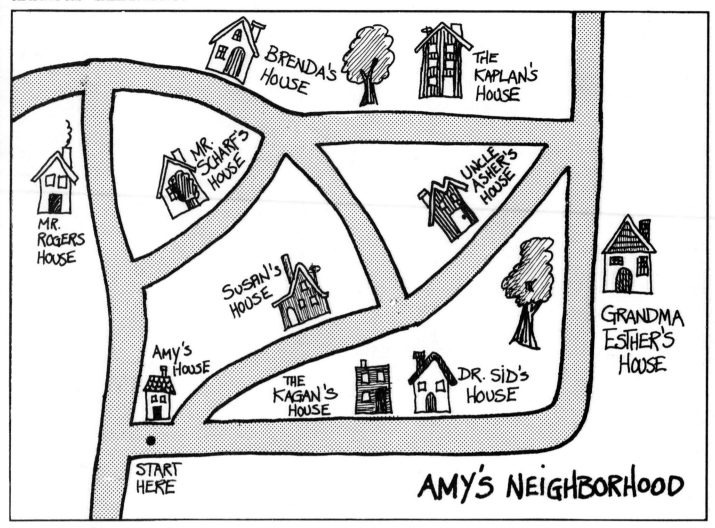

AMY'S NEIGHBORHOOD

HELP AMY DELIVER SHELAH MANOT

Amy's mother asked her to take the family *shelah manot* to six houses. She had to visit:

_____ Uncle Asher, the brother of Amy's father.

_____ The Kaplans, mother's best friends.

_____ Dr. Sid, the family dentist.

_____ Susan Steiner, Amy's best friend.

_____ Grandma Esther, the mother of Amy's mother.

_____ Mr. Scharf, Amy's Hebrew School teacher.

Look at this map. Draw the fastest way for Amy to make this trip. Number the stops on the trip.

A SHELAH MANOT PLAN

A *shelah manot* gift is made up of at least two kinds of food. Most families bake their own *shelah manot*. Fruit is also good for *shelah manot*.

List five things you might give as *shelach manot*.

1. _____
2. _____
3. _____
4. _____
5. _____

List five people who would be first on your *shelah manot* list.

1. _____
   _____ .
2. _____
   _____ .
3. _____
   _____ .
4. _____
   _____ .
5. _____

Decorate this *shelah manot* plate.

THE PURIM PROJECT

Rob didn't want to go. His mother and father made him do it. His mother said, "It is the right thing to do."His father said,"It is a *mitzvah*."It was all Mrs. Kelman's idea. She was his Hebrew School teacher. Rob had to do it because it was a school project.

Mrs. Kelman said: "It is a Jewish thing to do."She sent a letter home with every student. Rob brought the letter home. His mother read it and wrote her name on it. Rob brought it back to school. Then Mrs. Kelman wrote Rob's name on the Purim Project list. Now, he had to go.

The people working on the Purim Project met after Sunday School. Rob was scared. He didn't want to visit strangers. He didn't know what he would say. He just didn't want to go.

Five cars left the synagogue. Rob, David, Ari, Tamar and Heather went with Heather's mother. They had to make five stops. Mrs. Lurie was the last. It was Rob's turn to carry the plate of food up the stairs.

Mrs. Lurie was old. She lived alone. She smiled when she opened the door. Rob didn't have to say anything. Mrs. Lurie did a lot of talking. She brought everyone a cookie and a glass of water. She brought Heather's mother hot tea in a glass. She told the story of how she dressed as Esther when she was 7 years old. Her mother had to work all night to finish her costume. Rob liked Mrs. Lurie.

Rob wanted to see Mrs. Lurie again. Rob made his mother call Mrs. Lurie and invite her to dinner. His mother didn't want to do it. But Rob said, "It is a *mitzvah*." Then he said, "It is the right thing to do." At dinner, Mrs. Lurie sat next to Grandma Halperin. They liked each other.

After dinner everyone went to hear the reading of the *megillah*. Mrs. Lurie brought her own *gragger*. It was big and made of wood. Rob sat between Mrs. Lurie and Grandma Halperin. He had a good time. Mrs. Lurie made the most noise of anyone.

ANSWER THESE QUESTIONS:

1. Was Mrs. Lurie Rob's grandmother?   YES   NO
2. Was Rob afraid to visit Mrs. Lurie?   YES   NO
3. Were David, Ari, Tamar and Heather people Rob visited?   YES   NO
4. Did Rob's mother want to invite Mrs. Lurie?   YES   NO
5. What do we call "a Jewish thing to do?"_____
6. What *mitzvah* did the Purim Project perform? _____

   _____ .

7. What *mitzvah* did Rob and his family perform? _____

   _____ .

MATTANOT LE-EVYONIM—FAMILY

Tzedakah takes a lot of planning. To do a good job of giving *tzedakah* a person must learn about all the different people who are in need. One also has to learn about different ways of helping these people. Caring about *tzedakah* means being careful that the money you give does the most good.

Research these questions together. Parents should provide the direction needed to complete these questions and fill in the blanks. Use this exercise as an opportunity to talk about the commitment you have to helping others. This research can be the basis of your family's mattanot le-evyonim this Purim.

1. What is one organization which gives food to people who are hungry?

   _____ .

2. What is an organization which helps the homeless? _____

   _____ .

3. What is one organization which helps to cure people who are sick?

   _____ .

4. What is one of our family's favorite places to give *tzedakah*? _____

   _____ .

On Purim people dress up in costumes. Sometimes they become Mordechai, or Haman, or Esther or other people in the Purim story. Sometimes they dress up as other famous Jews. Other times they just wear strange costumes. Can you guess who each of these people is supposed to be?

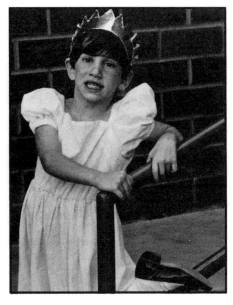

It isn't always easy to plan a good costume. It takes a lot of imagination. Look at these objects. Imagine what kind of costume could be made from each set.

aluminum foil, box, tube, ribbon, plate and hair brush.

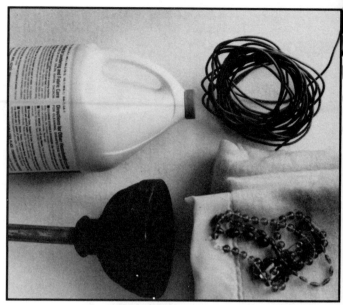

blanket, beads, bleach bottle, plunger and wire.

mop, rope, ladle, work glove and a piece of carpet.

bathrobe, basket, pot, pipe, brush and rain boots.

FOR THE PARENT
BUILDING JEWISH LIFE

A Partnership

This **Building Jewish Life** curriculum was designed in the belief that the best possible Jewish education happens only when the classroom and the home are linked. These pages are designed to cycle back and forth between those two realms, and to be used as a tool for learning in each. For this material to work most effectively, teacher and parent must assume interlocking roles and share in actualizing Jewish values and expressions. Each will do it in his/her own way. Each will do it with his/her own style. Together, they will reinforce each other, offering the child tangible experience and understanding of a visionary tradition.

Mitzvah Centered

Mitzvot is a word which means "commanded actions" and is used to describe a series of behaviors which Jewish tradition considers to be obligations. Classical Judaism teaches that the fabric of Jewish life is woven of 613 of these mandated actions. This series is built around the mitzvot, but it uses the term somewhat differently. In our day and age, the authority behind any "command" or obligation is a matter of personal faith and understanding. Each Jew makes his/her own peace or compromise with the tradition, affording it a place in his/her own life. In our age, the mitzvot have become rich opportunities. They are the things which Jews do, the activities by which we bring to life the ethics, insights, and wisdom of our Jewish heritage. Such acts as blessing holiday candles, visiting the sick, making a seder, comforting mourners, feeding the hungry, hearing the Purim megillah, studying Torah, educating our children, and fasting on Yom Kippur are all part of the mitzvah—Jewish-behavior—"opportunity" list. They are actions which, when they engage us, create moments of celebration, insight, and a sense of significance. It is through the mitzvot that the richness of the Jewish experience makes itself available. Without addressing the "authority" behind the mitzvot, and without assuming "obligation," this series will expose the power of many mitzvah-actions and advocate their performance based on the benefit they can bring to your family. It does so comfortably, because we know that you will explore this material and make decisions which are meaningful for you and your family.

The Classroom

In the classroom, this volume serves as a textbook. It helps the teacher introduce important objects, practices, personalities and places in Jewish life. It serves as a resource for exploring Jewish values and engages the students in "making meaning" from Jewish sources. The inclusion of both a

parent's guide and a teacher's guide at the end of this volume was an intentional act. We felt it was important for parents to fully understand what was being taught in the classroom.

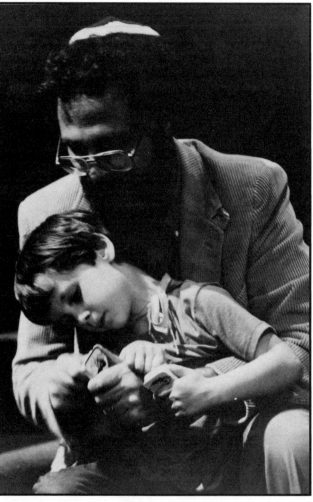

The Home

This material suggests three different levels of home involvement. On the simplest level, it contains a number of parent-child activities which demand your participation. They cannot be completed without your help. None of these are information-centered. The task of teaching names, pronunciations and facts has been left for the classroom. Rather, these are all moments of sharing values and insights or experimenting with the application of that which has been learned in class. They should be wonderful experiences and they call upon you to be a parent interested in his/her child, not a skilled teacher or tutor.

On a second level, much of this material can also be used to provide "read-aloud" experiences at bedtime, or as the basis for family study and discussion at the dinner table. Do not be afraid to "pre-empt" that which will be taught in class, or to "review" that which your child has learned. The more reinforcement, the better.

Finally, and most dramatically, there is the experience of participating in the mitzvot described in this book. We strongly urge you to make this a year to "try out" as many of them as possible. Think of them as the field trips and home experiments which will enrich the classroom experience and make it comprehensible.

The Network

The prime focus of this text series is celebration. Celebrations are better when they are shared with friends. New activities and new challenges are easier when they are shared. Familiar activities are also enriched by the presence of others. Many of the congregations which adopt this series will already have a system of Havurot, Jewish Holiday Workshops, or family activities. Others will organize parallel parent education sessions and special events for the families of the students in this program. We also imagine that some families will network with their friends to "try out" some of these mitzvah-events. It is our strong suggestion, that at least on an event-to-event basis, you connect with other Jewish families to experience some of the celebrations about which your child will be learning.

PURIM

Origins

Purim is a public victory celebration. Think of the old newsreels you've seen of the end of World War II, the street celebrations on VE-Day and VJ-Day. Or, remember the public ecstasy which follows a hometown World Series victory. There is a primal joy and release which comes with the end of a long struggle, which comes with a hard-fought victory.

Purim emerges from the national memory of an ancient victory. A stupid monarch is manipulated by a hateful minister. The genocide of the Jewish people is planned and given royal sanction. All seems lost. But then salvation comes, not from heaven, but from an assimilated Jewish woman who finds the courage to risk her life in order to save her people. Given her influence, royal opinion changes and the Jewish people are authorized to fight for their own lives. Purim is the celebration of their victory.

Scholars have long argued the historicity of these events. Much has been written about the identification of the book of Esther's King Ahasuerus as Xerxes I (486-465 B.C.E.), the fourth king of Persia's Achaemenidean kings. Some details match, some are contradictory; the historic reality of the book of Esther is unresolved. Regardless of the factual authenticity of the Purim story, it contains some important truths. In capsule form, we experience the many times the Jewish people have been redeemed from the brink of impending destruction. We relive our repeated encounters with irrational hate; we relearn the depth of our inner resolve to survive and prosper.

The book of Esther is a story of heroes. From an ancient biblical source, we learn an important non-sexist truth: women as well as men have shaped our destiny. Women, too, stand as models of courage and idealized behavior for all Jews. Also from that ancient source, a core lesson is learned about the difference one individual can make. Facing overwhelming odds, condemned by a seemingly omnipotent and irrational government, a woman who hid her Jewish identity in order to marry a king makes the difference by standing up to protect her people.

Four Opportunities

With the passage of time, this memory of redemption and victory became the foundation of a day of national celebration, the happiest day in the Jewish year. It became the one official "party day" in our year, the one time when nothing must be taken seriously. The Talmud uses the phrase *Ad de-lo yada* which means "not being able to tell the difference" as a definition of "legally drunk." On Purim it is a "legal" expectation that one *should* be drunk enough *"not to be able to tell the difference between* 'Cursed be Haman' *and* 'Blessed be Mordechai.'" For the usually hyper-self-conscious Jewish tradition, Purim is the one day of authorized (and almost total) abandon.

In his classic work on the theology of celebration, *The Feast of Fools*, Harvey Cox states, "In a success- and money-oriented society, we need a rebirth of patently unproductive festivity and expressive celebration...Festivity and fantasy are not only worthwhile in themselves, they are absolutely vital to human life. They enable man to relate himself to the past and the future in ways that seem impossible for animals. The *festival*, the special time when ordinary chores are set aside while man celebrates some events, affirms the sheer goodness of what is, or observes the memory of a god or hero, is distinctly human activity. It arises from man's peculiar power to incorporate into his own life the joys of other people and the experience of previous generations. Porpoises and chimpanzees may play. Only man celebrates. Festivity is a human form of play through which man appropriates an extended area of life, including the past, into his own experience."

Purim is our own ultimate festival, Judaism's own "feast of fools." As in the ironic juxtaposition of present slang, Purim is a day of "serious partying." In the Talmud we find the wonderfully ironic pun, *Yom* (the day) *Purim* (of Purim) *K'Yom* (is like the day) *Ha Kip-Purim* (the Day of Atonement). The year's most serious day and its least serious day are both necessary parts of our existence. Intensive self-examination and "serious partying" are both vital parts of the growth curve offered by the celebration-cycle of the Jewish year. Both are religious and spiritual epochs. Joking, the Kelemer Maggid explained, "On Purim, Jews dress up and masquerade as non-Jews, while on Yom Kippur they dress up and masquerade as pious Jews."

Four *mitzvot*/actions have become the essence of Purim.

The Reading of the *Megillah*. The central *mitzvah* of Purim is that of hearing the public reading of the book of Esther. Purim's festivities center around this act. The community gathers in costume, noisemakers in hand, prepared for this one activity. The carnivals, plays, special dinners and parties all follow from this moment.

The ritual for reading the *megillah* is patterned on that used for the Torah. Throughout the year, the public reading of the orah is the synagogue's dramatic high point. The formal ritual which surrounds that event proclaims the centrality of Torah learning in Jewish life. An honored reader uses a unique chant read words from a hand-crafted Torah scroll. To accentuate significance, the act is surrounded with blessings, one efore and one after. This pairing of blessings is unique, ecause all other Jewish ritual acts, except eating, require only ne *brakhah*. The analogy is clear; Torah learning is like ating; it is spiritual nourishment.

On Purim, the same elements are present in the *megillah* eading; a select reader chants from a handwritten text etween a pair of "before and after" *brakhot*. But on Purim, ere is a transformation. Instead of the usual quiet attention) "God's teachings," the masked mob interrupts the reading 'ith boisterous outbreaks; the pomp and circumstance of the ormal synagogue pageantry is shattered. Purim provides its wn unique way of teaching its lesson and values.

The *megillah* reading is a wonderful opportunity. If one took a child to synagogue only once a year, Purim would be ie best possible experience. Even without understanding the ontext, a child would immediately associate Judaism with ure joy and celebration. S/he would feel bonded to a people nd community who knew how to laugh, who loved their radition enough to play with it and enjoy it.

The actual story of the *megillah* is also an important esource. Its straightforward idealism, its belief that every Jew an be a hero and that an individual can make a difference, s one of the most important lessons we can teach our hildren. While particiption in the public event, the *megillah* eading, can positively influence your child's Jewish identity nd relationship to the Jewish people, time spent reading and liscussing the story of Esther can lead to a sense of self-worth nd real individual potential. It is the kind of mythic vision very would-be hero (male or female) needs.

The tradition asks Jews to study and hear the *megillah* each ear because of these two benefits. Purim is, after all, the noliday for children of every age. That is perhaps why the abbis taught (Midrash Mishle 9:2) that, vhile in Messianic times all other holidays vill be abolished, Purim will continue. That dea is found in the book of Esther itself, vhich tells us, "These days of Purim will never be forgotten among the Jewish people, nor the memory of these events ver vanish in their descendants." (9.28).

A Day of Celebration. The Talmud gives us a clue. It says,"When a person enters the month of Adar (the Hebrew month in which Purim falls), joy increases." (Ta'anit 29a). Joy and celebration are the central order of the day. Making Purim day into a celebration is Purim's second *mitzvah*. In the book of Esther, Mordechai commands the Jewish people to make the 14th of Adar into a day of "feasting and gladness." (9.22). From this verse, the rabbis made part of the celebration of Purim the particiaption in a *Purim Se'udah*, a festive Purim meal. It is a logical *mitzvah*. Jews have long applied the universal truth that the act of eating together is one of the best ways of defining a special event. In the past, this *Purim Se'udah* which took place without specific ritual on the

afternoon of Purim as the day was drawing to a close, was the location of much of the "serious-partying" which Purim demands. In previous generations, the *Purim Se'udah* ranked with the Passover Seder among the major family events in the annual social calender. It was here that legal limit of *ad de-lo-yada* was reached. In imitation of the great drinking-feasts which King Ahashuerus gave, the home was transformed into a regal palace, site of a great banquet. Costumes were worn. The children sang Purim songs and put on Purim plays. The playful mockery of traditional practice which characterized the public *megillah* reading extended into the home. At the *Purim Se'udah* upcoming Jewish comics got their start with inventive renditions of Kiddush and absurd Purim sermons. The *Purim Se'udah* was the private, family-centered, home expression of this public, nationalistic victory observance.

Today, Purim is almost exclusively a synagogue based experience. The *Purim Se'udah* has been upstaged by the Purim carnival. The public gathering for the *megillah* reading has been expanded with booths and games, prizes and dances. Other nouveau-*mitzvot*, those of buying a raffle ticket, wearing a costume, participating in congregational events, etc. have replaced the "*se'udah*" as the primary vehicles for celebration.

Whether it is done in public or in private, the chance to celebrate together is an important opportunity provided by Purim. Celebration is one of the prime bonding agents for both families and communities. Purim teaches us the role history and heritage play in our lives. It shows us that reflection upon our past can make us happy, that a more-than-2,000-year-old memory can still move us, affect our lives, and be a cause for celebration.

In addition, it provides the opportunity to teach our children how to "be happy." We live in an age where the art of having a good time is not obvious. In spite of, or because of, our technological advances, our celebrations often get out of hand. In a society where holiday crowds often break irrationally into riots, and where the use of 'recreational chemistry' (licit and illicit) is blatantly out of control, Purim is a chance to (1) model "how to party" reasonably and to (2) model appropriately the art of celebration.

The Giving of Shelah Manot. *Shelah Manot* is a simple *mitzvah*. It is just a matter of giving a gift of two or more kinds of food to the small circle of people you feel are important in your family's life. This too, is another act of celebration, rooted in a command Mordechai gave to the Jewish people after their victory. He said, "These days (Purim) should be observed as ... a time to send gifts to one another and presents to the poor." (Esther 9.22) There is nothing elaborate about *Shelah Manot*—a couple of hamantashen and a banana on a paper-plate specially decorated by your child, or a small basket filled with chocolate and some of your secret recipe cookies—but it provides another of Purim's wonderful opportunities. The mitzvah of *Shelah Manot* not only allows for the "joy of giving," but is intrinsically a statement of connection. The process of making a *Shelah Manot* list, preparing and delivering these gifts, is a wonderful way of identifying explicitly the family and community who influence your life. It is a wonderful way of teaching that "we are not alone." (Don't be afraid to be the first *Shelah Manot*-giver on your block....)

Mattanot le-Evyonim. One mark of the Jewish tradition's genius was its innate sense that every act of celebration, every moment of significance, every formal gathering should include an opportunity for giving *tzedakah*. *Tzedakah*, coming from a Hebrew root which means "justice," is the obligation to help those who are in need by sharing part of the wealth we have been fortunate enough to accumulate. From its ancient biblical roots, Judaism had a sense that participation in the total celebration which Purim offered would be a selfish act (and not a force for world-transformation) unless *tzedakah* were part of the process. The Bible instructs us that Mordechai and Esther themselves made *mattanot le-evyonim*, gifts to the poor, a Purim *mitzvah*.

For us, this is once again a wonderful opportunity. Too often, we hide the "good works" we do from our children. They see us drop a few token coins in various "pushkes," but the real commitments we make with our checkbooks are often hidden within the tedium of paying the monthly bills. Purim, with its *mitzvah* to send presents to the poor, is a perfect chance to make the whole family a part of deciding about and/or sending a portion of our annual charitable contributions. It is a wonderful time to share some of the things we really care about with our children. This, too, enhances the total celebration.

FOOTNOTES

1. Purim is a story of how good can defeat evil. The villain, Haman, is seen as archetypically evil. The Book of Esther establishes that he is totally wicked by introducing him as Haman, son of Hammedatha, the Agagite. For a person familiar with the biblical text, the name Agog sets off a warning buzzer. He was a King of the evil nation, Amalek. Amalek is the Torah's example of ultimate and total evil. In attacking the Israelites while they were in the wilderness, Amalek by-passed the warriors and slaughtered the elderly, the mothers and the young children who fell to the end of the line-of-march. It was an ancient act of genocide, and one which the Torah condemns. The Israelites (Ex. 17.14) are commanded to "blot out the name of Amalek." The collective act of making noise every time Haman's name is read is a symbolic way of literally fulfilling this command. The name of Haman, the Amalekite, is blotted out. Good destroys evil.

2. *Megillah* is a Hebrew word which means scroll. Many Jewish works are considered to be "scrolls." In the Bible we find a section called the five scrolls. It consists of *Song of Songs*, *Ruth*, *Lammentations*, *Ecclesiastes* and *Esther*. Each of these is considered to be a *megillah*. The labeling of *Megillat Esther* as the *megillah* is both a short-hand and the acknowledgement of its importance. The text of *Megillah* used on Purim is prepared in much the same was as the *Sefer Torah* used for public readings. It is handwritten on specially prepared parchment by a trained scribe. In reading it, however, we treat the *megillah* as if it were a letter, folding it, rather than rolling it. This custom reenacts the "decrees" that Mordechai sent to Jews throughout the kingdom, informing them of the situation.

3. *Esther* is one of the most confusing characters in Jewish history. She has been seen in two distinctly different ways. One interpretation sees her as a virtuous Jewess who follows all of God's commands, entering into a marriage with a non-Jewish monarch because it affords her the opportunity to save her people. The midrash weaves elaborate explanations of how she preserved her modesty, observed the dietary laws and retained her faith while in the harem. Conversely, another line of interpretation suggests that she was substantively assimilated, caring little for her Jewish background until circumstances forced her to act. The biblical text supports both visions. Wonderfully, the Jewess Hadassah takes the Persian name "Esther" which (predicated on a Hebrew root) means "hidden" and emerges to defeat evil. Whether the goodness, commitment and courage in Esther was intentionally or subconsciously hidden, her name completes the book's central metaphor. The book of Esther is the one book in the Bible where the name of God is not mentioned. Yet, as the rabbis regularly point out, God is indeed present in this story, "hidden in the actions of people created in God's image."

4. As we mentioned earlier in the parent's introduction, *mitzvah* is the central word in this series. *Mitzvah* is also an ideological word, its explanation often defining the boundary between the various branches of Judaism. Where your understanding of the concept of *mitzvah* is exact, the expression of a particular ideology of Jewish behavior, use and teach that understanding. In situations where your own ideology of Jewish practice is evolving, introduce *mitzvot* as "Jewish things to do," or "something which Jews do." Repeated context and examples will clarify its meaning more fully. The latter will allow children to relate to many different *mitzvah*-concepts.

5. *Purim*'s name comes from the statement in the book of Esther that Haman "threw lots/*Purim*" to determine the date for the annihilation of the Jewish people. While in our mind, the word "lots" conjures up a bingo kind of number pulling, the biblical description suggests the casting of an oracle, something resembling the *I Ching*. In a symbol of victory, the act of dooming the Jewish people was transformed into the name of their celebration of triumph.

6. Maimonides was a 12th and 13th century Jewish scholar who wrote one of the most important codes of Jewish law, the *Mishneh Torah*. In the law quoted, he teaches that *mattanot le-evyonim* is the most important of Purim's *mitzvot*, taking priority over personal Purim dinners and gifts to friends. He concludes the law with the statement that this act (like all acts of *tzedakah*) is important because it represents the best of what we can be, and helps us live up to the image in which we were created, God's image (Gen. 1.27)

OR THE TEACHER

The Purim volume of **Building Jewish Life** centers on three objectives:

1. Students will master the basic vocabulary of the celebration of Purim consisting of the words listed in the Essential Vocabulary section below.

2. Students will learn, act out, and be able to tell the story of the Esther, including the ability to identify Esther, Mordechai, King Ahasuerus and Haman.

3. Students will learn about, practice, be able to explain, and participate in the four *mitzvot* of Purim: hearing the *megillah*, making a celebration, sending *shelah manot* (food gifts to friends), and giving *mattanot le-evyonim* (Purim *Tzedakah*).

ESSENTIAL VOCABULARY

1. *Gragger/Ra'ashan*   Purim Noisemaker
2. *Megillah*   Hebrew for scroll, short for *Megillat Esther*, the scroll of the Book of Esther
3. *Hamantashen*   Purim cookie named after Haman
4. *Shelaḥ Manot*   *Mitzvah* of sending Purim food gifts to friends
5. *Mattanot Le-evyonim*   *Mitzvah* of giving Purim *Tzedakah*
6. *Purim Spiel*   Play of the story of the Book of Esther

ADDITIONAL VOCABULARY

1. *Brachot*   Blessings
2. Hero
3. Celebration
4. Decree
5. Imitating
6. Sackcloth

We will assume that this material will cover four classroom sessions. Teachers should feel free to adapt and improvise according to (1) time available, (2) age and ability of students, (3) involvement of families, (4) previous background, and (5) moments of inspiration.

LESSON ONE

1. **SET INDUCTION**: BRING in a *gragger*, a *megillah*, and some *hamantashen*. USE these objects to introduce the celebration of PURIM. READ pages 1-7 of this book with your students.

2. **PRESENTING THE PURIM STORY**: TELL/REVIEW the story of Purim. USE masks, props, puppets, dolls, etc. to make the story exciting. USE pages 28-31, the fill-in-the-blanks and coloring exercises, to REINFORCE the story.

3. **MAKING A GRAGGER**: MAKE your own GRAGGERS. Any good container: Pringle cans, Band-Aid boxes, food containers, or a paper plate folded in half and stapled closed, can be filled with stones, beads or marbles and then decorated with Contact paper, crayons or stickers.

DISCUSS the idea on page 1. ASK: How does the *gragger* teach us that "when we work together, we are stronger than evil." ALLOW students to share their ideas. DON'T look for one correct answer.

4. **USING THE GRAGGERS**: PRACTICE hearing the *megillah*. READ part of the Purim Spiel (pages 11 ff) or the real *megillah*. Have students MAKE NOISE every time Haman's name is read.

5. **HOMEWORK**: ASSIGN students page 32, the exercise

about Heroes, to do *with their parents*. You may want (1) to send a note home explaining the assignment, and (2) to have students and parents MAKE A POSTER of both heroes (rather than just fill in the page in the book).

6. CLOSURE: REVIEW the major things learned: THE NAMES Ahasuerus, Mordechai, Esther and Haman. THE OBJECTS: *Gragger*, *Hamantashen* and *Megillah*.

LESSON TWO

1. SET INDUCTION: Have students SHARE the heroes they wrote about with their parents. ASK: "What makes someone a hero?" ANSWER: "A hero is someone you want to be like." DISCUSS: "How do we want to be like Mordechai and Esther?"

2. TEXT READING: TELL the class that next week they are going to be part of a play of the Purim story. This week they are going to look at the script. READ pages 11-22 with the class. STOP to discuss some of the major questions at the bottom of the page. *Feel free to adjust the amount of the story you cover and the number of questions you ask to time available and your class' attention span.*

3. ACTING OUT THE STORY: AFTER you have read and studied the story, spend some time "acting out" some of the situations. USE the *pretend* sections at the bottom of the page as your guide. HAVING costumes and props available will help this work and be lots of fun.

4. THE FOUR MITZVOT: INTRODUCE the four *mitzvot* of Purim. USE pages 8 and 9, 23-27 to reinforce this material. Have the class COMPLETE the map on page 34 as a reinforcement.

5. HOMEWORK: ASSIGN parents and children to work on page 35.

6. CLOSURE: REVIEW the four mitzvot of Purim. ASK students to explain (a) what we do, and (b) what we learn from HEARING the *megillah*, MAKING Purim a celebration, (c) SENDING Shelah Manot, and (d) GIVING Mattanot Le-Evyonim.

LESSON THREE

If at all possible, invite parents to join the class for this session.

1. MAKING HAMANTASHEN: PREPARE cookie dough in advance. HAVE students (a) roll dough, (2) cut circles, (3) fill with fillings, and (4) fold three sides in to make a triangle. BAKE in oven. SAVE for the end of class. You may also want to decorate plates for *Shelah Manot*. If parents have not been invited to attend this session, provide a piece of fruit to go with the Hamantashen and send it home as a "practice" *shelah manot*.

2. REHEARSAL OF PURIM SPIEL: ASSIGN students (and parents) to produce each scene in the Purim Spiel. Each page in the book represents 1 scene. ALLOW them time to REHEARSE and MAKE costumes and props. OFFICIALLY AUTHORIZE improvization—"making new things up."

3. PERFORMANCE OF SPIEL: HAVE GROUPS present their scenes.

4. READING A STORY: BREAK class into small groups. MAKE sure that at least one adult is with each group. Have them READ and DISCUSS the story on page 36-37. The last two questions are tricky. The mitzvah performed by the Purim project could either be *shelah manot* or *mattanot le-evyonim*. The *mitzvah* performed by Rob's family is not in the book, it is called *hakhnassat orahim*, providing hospitality. It is okay for students and parents to struggle with these. It will expand their vision of the "*mitzvah*-system."

5. HOMEWORK: ASSIGN page 35. PARTY: CONCLUDE the day with a celebration.

LESSON FOUR

1. SET INDUCTION: HAVE students share some of the "research" they did on places where they could give *mattanot le- evyonim* as homework with their parents. CONSTRUCT a master list of all suggestions on a piece of paper. SEND the complete list home at the end of the day.

2. REVIEW THE FOUR PURIM MITZVOT: HAVE students work on a mural which shows all four activities.

3. PRACTICE ALL THESE MITZVOT: READ a piece of the "real" book of Esther and have students RESPOND to Haman's name. If possible, invite the rabbi, educator or cantor to practice with your class. SEND *shelah manot* to someone, or some other class. (Perhaps the teacher they had last year). DISCUSS where to send your *Keren Ami* as a *matatnot le-evyonim*. END with a *Se'udat Purim*. Have a great Purim party.